CONTENTS

THE SUBMISSION

As we have said at the beginning of the other books in these series; we are presenting this disclaimer to make sure we understand that we are trying to understand to the best of our ability something that is pretty much impossible. Realize that this is our best effort to make sense of something that is slightly, if not tremendously above or our capability to understand. There are huge aspects of this that we cannot understand. We are trying to understand something intangible; we do not get to see, touch, or interact with it in a physical way. We are seeking the truth and understanding of what is the actual scriptural; we are not necessarily seeking comfort or reassurance. Now, we are continuing in our quest in trying to understand what the Ruach Ha Kodesh is; with that being said, let us go to John 6:47-50, "Verily, verily, I say unto you, He that believeth on me hath everlasting life." Verse 48, "I am that bread of life." Verse 49, "Your fathers did eat manna in the wilderness, and are dead." Verse 50, "This is the bread which cometh down from heaven, that a man may eat thereof, and not die."

He is making a comparison between what was happening in the Exodus and what is going on here; comparing this physical bread with this metaphor, He is trying to give us here. He was not talking about literally cannibalizing him. Moving on, verse 51-53, reads, "I am the living bread which came down from heaven: if any man eat of this bread, he shall live forever: and the bread that I will give is my flesh, which I will give for the life of the world." Verse 52, "The Jews therefore strove among themselves, saying, How can this man give us his flesh to eat?" Verse 53, "Then YAHUSHUA said unto them, Verily, verily, I say unto you, Except ye eat the flesh of the Son of man, and drink his blood, ye have no life in you." No doubt, this sounded strange to the audience; remember this is a Hebrew Israelite audience. He is telling them to some degree what their history is and that they do not understand what happened in their past, and He is trying to put it in a different perspective. He is trying to get through their paradigms and give them this whole metaphor to shift everything in their heads. Look at verses 54-59, which reads, "Whoso eateth my flesh, and drinketh my blood, hath eternal life; and I will raise him up at the last day." Verse 55, "For my flesh is meat indeed, and my blood is drink indeed." Verse 56, "He that eateth my flesh, and drinketh my blood, dwelleth in me, and I in him." Verse 57, "As the living Father hath sent me, and I live by the Father: so, he that eateth me, even he shall live by me." Verse 58, "This is that bread which came down from heaven: not as your fathers did eat manna, and are dead: he that eateth of this bread shall live forever." Verse 59, "These things said he in the synagogue, as he taught in Capernaum." So, He is talking to Hebrew Israelites in a synagogue; one of the metaphors we can see is He bringing us back to an event that happened when Moses brought Israel out of Egypt. Now, what happened along the way, was they got this thing called, Manna and were being taught about the Sabbath; they had not gotten to Sinai yet. The word, Manna in Hebrew means, what is this?

Something else happened when they got to Sinai; there was the bread that came out of heaven; YAHUAH gave them the Commandments; the Torah. That is what is linked to life; we are going to examine this more closely; by the way, in Deuteronomy, we are told that we are not to live by bread alone; but by every word that comes out of the mouth of YAHUAH. Look at Deuteronomy 8:3, it reads, "And he humbled thee, and suffered thee to hunger, and fed thee with manna, which thou knewest not, neither did thy fathers know; that he might make thee know that man doth not live by bread only, but by every word that proceedeth out of the mouth of YAHUAH doth man live." This is what gave them life; this is what they needed to live by; He is linking Himself to that - Torah. Of course, they are thinking your flesh; your blood; they are confused. Continuing, go to John 6:61-65, which reads, "When YAHUSHUA knew in himself that his disciples murmured at it, he said unto them, Doth this offend you?" Verse 62, "What and if ye shall see the Son of man ascend up where he was before?"

We are going to link the Ruach. Verse 63, "It is the Spirit that quickeneth; the flesh profiteth nothing: the words that I speak unto you, they are Spirit, and they are life." We could stop here, and Christianity probably does; but they are missing the point. The point is; the words that I speak to you are Spirit and life. This can get into that ethereal Spirit that Christianity likes to get into; if they do not listen to the rest of the verse. Some of you may have heard of or were taught that way. However, He is saying; the Spirit gives life. Not the Trinity; there is not the third part of the Trinity; there is no Trinity. He is not talking about that; He tells you exactly what He is saying; read a little more. Link that back to what to He is saying, that which came down from heaven; the Torah. This is where we go back to our loop, that we like to use in John 14:6, where YAHUSHUA says, I am the truth, and Psalm 119:142,160; where both are saying the Torah or the word is the truth. Then if you go back to John 1:14; it says, that the word or the Torah put on flesh; there is your loop. YAHUSHUA is the walking, talking, living Torah; so, of course, His words, which come out of the essence of who and what He is; our life and they are Spirit, truth, the Torah. It is the same thing that came down from heaven; when He talks about that which comes down from heaven; He is referring to Himself. He is also referring to the Torah; He is giving them a deeper understanding of what happened in Exodus 20, and that is what we need to comprehend; the linkage between these things. However, if you are not studied; the Spirit of the Ruach cannot link those things. The Ruach is supposed to bring to remembrance; make connections; be the teacher; not direct downloads; not spontaneous knowledge; it is connecting what you have. If you are not liking what you are getting there is limitations in your connections; you have not put enough in; you are not studying your book enough; you are not giving it enough raw material to work with. You cannot connect the dots, and the word will not make any sense.

Verse 64, "But there are some of you that believe not. For YAHUSHUA knew from the beginning who they were that believed not, and who should betray him." Verse 65, "And he said, Therefore said I unto you, that no man can come unto me, except it were given unto him of my Father." So, stop knocking on doors in the morning and waking people up; trying to get them to come to YAHUSHUA. He says, no one can come to me unless it has been given to Him by my Father. It is not your job to go finding and chasing them down; if the Father is drawing them; they will be seeking and searching for someone to give them some answers. If they come across you hopefully you are trained and ready, but be careful whatever you give them; if it is wrong then that is on you, and there is an overabundance of people out there very happy to provide you with incorrect information. Some of them do not know it is wrong because they have not been trained; they have not gone through enough training. If you have been walking this walk out two, three, four, or five years; you have not walked it long enough to know what you do not know. Just because you keep the observances and you fixed how you eat; does not give you the doctrinal stuff; the positional stuff is much tougher to unravel; the lexicon, you do not realize how messed up your lexicon is. In other words, you read a word, you think you know what it means, and it is entirely upside-down and backward. Before you read the teaching on Grace; it had you entirely upside-down, inside-out. No understanding of what the Kadosh (Holy Spirit) was; churches and the backgrounds that you all have did not do a good job giving you the definition of the terms; the lexicon; you are not going to realize all of that in the first three, four, or five years. Now you can accelerate the process by finding an anointed, appointed teacher, who can start feeding that into you and accelerate the process; but if you are fishing for it on your own, it is going to take longer.

We should always be growing in knowledge and growing in understanding. You are familiar with the verse that says, growing in grace? However, if you do not know what grace is; that does not help you very much. If you think you know, when you are wrong; that does not help you very much either. So, let us stick to growing your knowledge and understanding; you should be improving and increasing in that overtime, clarity should be coming in overtime; errors should be weeded out over time; that is a good metaphor; the weeding out. You do not realize how many weeds are growing on your lawn; doing this a couple of years, and you think you have got this perfect lawn; the indoctrination, the misdirection, the deceiving that the enemy has done through the church system is so pervasive. Through you, it is going to take you a long time even to realize the tendrils that are still there that you think you have gotten rid of; these false doctrines are insidious.

Let us reread John 6:65-66, which read, "And he said, Therefore said I unto you, that no man can come unto me, except it were given unto him of my Father." Here is the scary part; verse 65, "From that time many of his disciples went back, and walked no more with him." His students; not just people that heard of him. It says his taught ones would not walk with Him anymore. So, we should not be upset when people do not walk with us; we are not comparing ourselves to Him; but even His own taught ones would not walk with Him after they could not handle some of the things He said. Moving on, verse 66-67, "From that time many of his disciples went back, and walked no more with him." Verse 67, "Then said YAHUSHUA unto the twelve, Will ye also go away?" Remember, this is not the twelve; He had more students than that. Verse 68, "Then Simon Peter answered him, Lord, to whom shall we go? thou hast the words of eternal life." This is the place we need to get eventually; the words of everlasting means, you have things that you say that if we understand them and do them will lead to everlasting life.

It is not like the words are an incantation in magic; like if you say these words tonight, you will live forever; He is saying you must have the understanding and knowledge. It is in your words you explain, teach, and give information that leads to everlasting life. Verse 69-70, read, "And we believe and are sure that thou art the Messiah, the Son of the living ELOHIM." Verse 70, "YAHUSHUA answered them, Have not I chosen you twelve, and one of you is a devil?" We need to embrace verse 68, all of us should be able to say, master to where we are going to go. If you have found a teacher, and you find that other teachers are saying something different than your teacher; go to your teacher and clarify it. Do not allow others to cause a stumbling block between you and your teacher. If you are hearing truths that make you decide that you no longer want that teacher; fine; go and find yourself another teacher, however, as long as that one is your teacher; you need to respect his teachings and go to that teacher. Let us go into the specific part of verse 68 when it says, even in the understanding of this master to whom shall we go? Let us understand that this is a discipleship process; something that has not been taught for 2,000 years. Assuming it was taught reasonably well for the first hundred or so years after YAHUSHUA was resurrected. We lost this whole discipleship thing, and He is saying, you are my students, and I am teaching you; you recognize all of that; do you want to leave me? It is not just Him saying do you want to leave me, as the Son of the Father; do you want to leave me as YAHUAH in the flesh? Do you no longer wish to be discipled by me? He answered and said, master, where can we go? Who's is going to give us the words of life? If you have found a teacher that possesses the words of like; in other words, understands what YAHUSHUA has said, and can teach you what YAHUSHUA meant, and what He was doing. You have to do self-reflection and ask Can this man give you the words of life you need to say the same thing? Where would I go? Who else is out there teaching this? Sadly, there is such a wide variety of false doctrines that are being taught; it is hard to find teachers teaching the same thing. Your teacher should be teaching you YAHUSHUA; showing you YAHUSHUA; giving you words of life. As one who disciples you as a disciple should be taught about his teacher; to lead you in His direction. A conduit, if anybody is out there trying to promote anything else; it is nonsense. They should be pointing you towards an understanding of his teacher; who ultimately is still your teacher. He works through people; when people were in congregations led by Paul, or by Peter, or any of the other disciples who were sent out to lead Israel back into the covenant; they were saying I want to teach you about my teacher YAHUSHUA. They were not saying I want to introduce you to Him and leave you on your own. Telling you this Spirit or Holy spirit was going to come and tell you everything you needed to know. Now, we need somebody to share and to give discernment, and understanding; put the pieces of the puzzle together; that is called teaching and instruction; that is scriptural. There are supposed to be Torah teachers; there is no scriptural basis for you just being self-taught. Zero, there was always supposed to be those who were teaching. Even the teacher is supposed to be learning from others; as well as from the Ruach to help filter through things. The problem is you still have to do the verification; they may have done the heavy lifting, but you have to study it for yourself and make sure that it is what they claim. Many people are presenting their speculation as a fact; do not accept that; do not let them get away with it.

Continuing, let us go to John 7:33, we are starting to see that YAHUSHUA is referring to the Spirit, and it is not an entity. He is saying my words are Spirit. Note: there is a point in scripture where it talks about the Father seeking those that will worship Him in Spirit, and truth; now, this connects up to John 6; see, YAHUSHUA said, my words are Spirit, and he has told you, I am the truth. He is saying the Father is seeking those that will worship Him in the fullness of YAHUSHUA; understanding, His words and understanding that He is the truth. My hypothesis is, that truth means, the mechanics of it; Spirit means the fullness of the intent. So, in short, what it is saying here is, the Spirit; the fullness of the intent that gives life; the mechanics does not give you life. Doing the work within the context of the fullness of the intent does lead to life. He explains this in His first messages in Matthew when he says, you have heard of old not to commit adultery, but I am telling you the fullness of the intent was that you would not even lust. So, the mechanical thing of saying, well, I am okay, never committed adultery; but you dreamed about it; so that does not bring life. So, when He says in John, this connects up to where it says; worship Him in Spirit and in truth; He says, my words are Spirit; I want you to worship through me to worship the Father in YAHUSHUA's words; in His context of truth; by walking and living it out. Now in John 7:33-35, "Then said YAHUSHUA unto them, Yet a little while am I with you, and then I go unto Him that sent me." So, this is continuing similar though to where He was in John 6; verse 34, "Ye shall seek Me, and shall not find Me: and where I am, thither ye cannot come."

Verse 35, "Then said the Jews among themselves, Whither will He go, that we shall not find Him? will He go unto the dispersed among the Gentiles, and teach the Gentiles?" The Hebrews understood that the Messiah was going to have a message to go out to those Israelites that were scattered abroad outside of the borders of Israel. Verses 36-37, reads, " What manner of saying is this that He said, Ye shall seek Me, and shall not find Me: and where I am, thither ye cannot come?" Verse 37, "In the last day, that great day of the feast, YAHUSHUA stood and cried, saying, If any man thirst, let him come unto Me, and drink." This is likely a day that is referred to often as the last day; the great day of the feast; Sukkot is not eight days; it is seven; the eighth day is a separate festival called the last great day or the eighth-day festival. So, this likely happened at the end of Sukkot. Verses 38, "He that believeth on Me, as the scripture hath said, out of his belly shall flow rivers of living water." Realize this is still connecting to John when He said if you drink of My blood; eat of My flesh. That is giving a bit more clarity of what it means by drinking; He says if anyone thirsts let him come to me and let him who believes in me drink. He is quoting scripture; out of His innermost shall flow rivers of living water. Now, let us take a side excursion here; dealing with the rivers of living water. But, first let us finish these last two verses; verse 39, " (But this spake He of the Spirit, which they that believe on Him should receive: for the Holy Ghost was not yet given; because that YAHUSHUA was not yet glorified.)" Verse 40, "Many of the people therefore, when they heard this saying, said, Of a truth this is the Prophet." This is a crucial point; now let us go on this little journey connecting the dots. He is saying, this idea about these rivers of living water and He is connecting it up to say that this was concerning the Ruach or Spirit; so where He says, "...which was not yet given..." now where we end up may take you by surprise; it is not referring to Acts 2; we will see that when we look at the verses that talk about the rivers of living water. Hint: This is talking about when He returns; this is talking about the 2nd coming of YAHUSHUA. However, everybody has taken this verse to think He was talking about Acts 2; it is connected to the previous verse which talks about, out of His innermost shall flow rivers of living water; we have to understand that first before we can understand what He is talking about concerning the Spirit. He said, "...out of his belly shall flow rivers of living water." We have to be careful that we follow the sentences. He says and "*this*"; that is the keyword; we have to know what "*this*" is if anyone thirsts let him come to Me and let him who believes in Me drink; as

the scripture said out of His belly shall flow rivers of living water. That's
what He just said it is speaking about the Holy Spirit. So, delete; erase
everything you ever understood about this being connected to in Acts 2;
along with everything else you may have believed. Let us see what it is
connected to by reading in the Tanakh the verses about the rivers of living
water flowing out of His belly; He knows and said He is quoting as the
scripture says, so, it is not He said something we assume; it is from the
scripture. This is about the Ruach; from scripture. But, first let us understand
why they thought He was, "the" Prophet.
Go to Deuteronomy 18:13-22, we have something that explains that they
were looking for one known as, "the" Prophet not a Prophet. Even though in
speculation some thought He was Elijah; some thought He was Jeremiah or
Isaiah; but here is the Prophet that Moses mentions in verse 13-22, " Thou
shalt be perfect with YAHUAH thy ELOHIM." Verse 14, "For these nations,
which thou shalt possess, hearkened unto observers of times, and unto
diviners: but as for thee, YAHUAH thy ELOHIM. hath not suffered thee so
to do." Verse 15, "YAHUAH thy ELOHIM will raise up unto thee a Prophet
from the midst of thee, of thy brethren, like unto Me; unto Him ye shall
hearken;" I believe this is who the people were referring to; I cannot prove it;
However, I believe that is what they meant when they said, truly is this the
Prophet.
Continuing, verse 16, "According to all that thou desiredst of YAHUAH thy
ELOHIM. in Horeb in the day of the assembly, saying, Let me not hear again
the voice of YAHUAH my ELOHIM, neither let me see this great fire any
more, that I die not." Verse 17, "And YAHUAH said unto me, They have
well spoken that which they have spoken." Verse 18, "I will raise them up a
Prophet from among their brethren, like unto thee, and will put My words in
His mouth; and He shall speak unto them all that I shall command him."
Verse 19, "And it shall come to pass, that whosoever will not hearken unto
My words which He shall speak in my name, I will require it of him." Verse
20, "But the prophet, which shall presume to speak a word in My name,
which I have not commanded Him to speak, or that shall speak in the name of
other gods, even that prophet shall die." Verse 21, "And if thou say in thine
heart, How shall we know the word which YAHUAH hath not spoken?"
Verse 22, "When a prophet speaketh in the name of YAHUAH, if the thing
follow not, nor come to pass, that is the thing which YAHUAH hath not
spoken, but the prophet hath spoken it presumptuously: thou shalt not be

afraid of him." Remember, Hebraic understanding is cyclical with an ultimate fulfillment. So, yes, Moses is speaking about Isaiah, Jeremiah, Ezekiel, and every one of the prophets. When they spoke, and they did not listen, it was required of them. He is even speaking of Joshua; who was also allowed to be in that position to lead them and speak the words of YAHUAH. Ultimately, there was a fulfillment of the one called, "the" Prophet or Hebraically they understood they were looking for one known as "the" Prophet like unto Moses. They were speculating here that YAHUSHUA was this man. For all of you that are running around listening to everybody and anybody; there is no reason for you to continue to follow anyone of the Hebrew Israelite teachers that have named dates of the end times and it came not. What did we just read? He said, when the Prophet speaks, the person who claims he is speaking on behalf of YAHUAH and it does not happen; it comes not; that is not the word of YAHUAH. We are reading what it says in the Bible; the word is true.

Moving on, so, this is them; understanding, thinking, and believing in what we are reading in John; the YAHUSHUA might be this Prophet, that Moses was telling him about in Deuteronomy 18; with that; now let us look at the verses that deal with the flowing of the rivers of living water. Go to Isaiah 44:1-4, " Yet now hear, O Jacob my servant; and Israel, whom I have chosen:" Verse 2, "Thus saith YAHUAH that made thee, and formed thee from the womb, which will help thee; Fear not, O Jacob, my servant; and thou, Jesurun, whom I have chosen." Verse 3, "For I will pour water upon him that is thirsty, and floods upon the dry ground: I will pour My spirit upon thy seed, and My blessing upon thine offspring:" Verse 4, "And they shall spring up as among the grass, as willows by the water courses." Now, this does not say exactly what YAHUSHUA quoted, yet some verses will; we are just building an understanding of how YAHUAH uses this idea. Bear in mind, He never mentions anybody else being chosen but Israel; Israel is the chosen. They did not lose the promise, and the ridiculous doctrine of the "churches are the chosen" or some other way that people want to make it up; it has always been about His people Israel.

Romans 11 is about the grafting in of the scattered Hebrew Israelites. Moving on, reread Isaiah 44:3, it said, "For I will pour water upon him that is thirsty, and floods upon the dry ground: I will pour my spirit upon thy seed, and my blessing upon thine offspring:" This is prophetically about the end times of the bringing back together; the regathering of the Hebrew Israelites into New

Jerusalem. He is speaking about the future end times because that is the "blessings" in full poured upon the offspring of Israel. He is saying do not worry about the fact that you are suffering and have all of these problems right now; there will be a time when your seed; your descendants will have this living water. He said I am going to pour My Spirit on your seed; this water poured out on the thirsty. I am going to pour my Spirit on your seed because the Spirit is going to feed them if they are starving, thirsty, and parched. It is the words of YAHUSHUA; it is the words of YAHUAH. Hold on to that thought, and let us go to Jeremiah 2:13, "For my people have committed two evils; they have forsaken me the fountain of living waters, and hewed them out cisterns, broken cisterns, that can hold no water." We see again, YAHUAH referring to himself as a fountain of living water; the source of the living waters; that is what YAHUSHUA said. Go to Jeremiah 17:13, " O YAHUAH, the hope of Israel, all that forsake thee shall be ashamed, and they that depart from me shall be written in the earth, because they have forsaken YAHUAH, the fountain of living waters." Here again, YAHUAH pointed out that He is the fountain of living waters. Read verses 14-15, "Heal me, O YAHUAH, and I shall be healed; save me, and I shall be saved: for thou art my praise." Verse 15, "Behold, they say unto me, Where is the word of the Lord? let it come now." Again, that last verse connects the fountain of living waters and the word of YAHUAH; they are looking for the water, but they are looking for the word. The water and the word are connected; over and over again; just like the Spirit and the water, and the word is now connected. YAHUSHUA has said, My words are Spirit, and He is saying out of Me is going to flow the rivers of living water; the word is going to go forth from Zion. The word of YAHUAH from Jerusalem; it is all the same thing; let us not confuse this.

Go now to Zechariah 14:1-2, 4, 8, let us first understand the timeframe, it reads, "Behold, the day of the YAHUAH cometh, and thy spoil shall be divided in the midst of thee." Verse 2, "For I will gather all nations against Jerusalem to battle; and the city shall be taken, and the houses rifled, and the women ravished; and half of the city shall go forth into captivity, and the residue of the people shall not be cut off from the city." Verse 4, "And his feet shall stand in that day upon the Mount of Olives, which is before Jerusalem on the east, and the mount of Olives shall cleave in the midst thereof toward the east and the west, and there shall be a very great valley; and half of the mountain shall remove toward the north and half of it toward the south." This is when His feet shall stand on the Mount of Olives, and it is going to split in two; this has not happened yet; now, in the context of that end time; verse 8-9, "And it shall be in that day, that living waters shall go out from Jerusalem; half of them toward the former sea, and half of them toward the hinder sea: in summer and in winter shall it be." Verse 9, "And YAHUAH shall be King over all the earth: in that day shall there be one YAHUAH, and his name one." Do you see the connection? The water flows to something that has not happened yet; you see a hint to it. There is more, go to Psalm 36:8-9, "They shall be abundantly satisfied with the fatness of thy house; and thou shalt make them drink of the river of thy pleasures." Verse 9, "For with thee is the fountain of life: in thy light shall we see light." Again, connecting it back to YAHUAH; this is all going into the future. Go to Proverbs 14:26-27, it reads, "In the fear of YAHUAH is strong confidence: and his children shall have a place of refuge." Verse 27, "The fear of YAHUAH is a fountain of life, to depart from the snares of death." The fountain of life protecting you from death, and it is linked not to the fear of YAHUAH. The waters; this fountain is like the Spirit being linked to the word; which is linked to the Torah. We are connecting it all; they are not separate things; they are talking about one thing. Now, let us go over to 1 Corinthians 10:1-6, "Moreover, brethren, I would not that ye should be ignorant, how that all our fathers were under the cloud, and all passed through the sea;" Verse 2, "And were all baptized unto Moses in the cloud and in the sea;" Verse 3, "And did all eat the same spiritual meat;" Verse 4, "And did all drink the same spiritual drink: for they drank of that spiritual Rock that followed them: and that Rock was Messiah." Verse 5, "But with many of them ELOHIM was not well pleased: for they were overthrown in the wilderness." Verse 6, "Now these things were our examples, to the intent we should not lust after evil things, as they also lusted." There was something in this whole thing that He is relating us to waters, sea, life, but those that chose evil chose death and were "overthrown in the wilderness", those that chose light, life drank of "that spiritual Rock that followed them"; what did Moses say when he brought down the commandments from YAHUAH? I lay before you life and death; choose life.

What are life and word? The Torah; the instructions that teach you how to love your Creator; how to love each other. It is the two great commandments; to love Him and to love each other as Israelites; it is the rest of it that explains how to do it. He gives us specific details on how to love Him and how to love

each other. Those two categories of what He wants us to know is what He expects us to do in terms of relating with Him, and what He expects us to do when relating to each other as a nation. Now, go to Revelation 7:13-17, it reads, "And one of the elders answered, saying unto me, What are these which are arrayed in white robes? and whence came they?" Verse 14, "And I said unto him, Sir, thou knowest. And he said to me, These are they which came out of great tribulation, and have washed their robes, and made them white in the blood of the Lamb." Verse 15, "Therefore are they before the throne of YAHUAH, and serve Him day and night in His temple: and He that sitteth on the throne shall dwell among them." Verse 16, "They shall hunger no more, neither thirst anymore; neither shall the sun light on them, nor any heat." Verse 17, "For the Lamb which is in the midst of the throne shall feed them, and shall lead them unto living fountains of waters: and ELOHIM shall wipe away all tears from their eyes." Hopefully, you can see the Lamb, YAHUSHUA shall provide them with the fountains of water of life. Again, this has not happened yet; this is at the end of this world and the beginning of the new world to come; hold that thought; let us go to Revelation 21:6-7, "And He said unto me, It is done. I am Alpha and Omega, the beginning and the end. I will give unto him that is athirst of the fountain of the water of life freely." Verse 7, "He that overcometh shall inherit all things; and I will be his ELOHIM, and he shall be my son."
Moving on, go to Revelation 22:1, it reads, "And He shewed me a pure river of water of life, clear as crystal, proceeding out of the throne of ELOHIM and of the Lamb." Drop down to verse 7:37-39, "And the Spirit and the bride say, Come. And let him that heareth say, Come. And let him that is athirst come. And whosoever will let him take the water of life freely." Now, go back to John 7, now that we have that background; let the Ruach connect the dots for you as we read this; remember in chapter 6; He has already talked about being the bread of life, and to drink of His blood. You will not have life, but whoever drinks of my blood will have everlasting life. Now, verse 37, "In the last day, that great day of the feast, YAHUSHUA stood and cried, saying, If any man thirst, let him come unto Me, and drink." Verse 38, "He that believeth on Me, as the scripture hath said, out of His belly shall flow rivers of living water." Verse 39, "(But this spake He of the Spirit, which they that believe on Him should receive: for the set-apart Spirit was not yet given; because that YAHUSHUA was not yet glorified.)" They were about to receive; to some level; fullness of understanding; opening up their

understanding; so, yes, there is a previous and continuous manifestation; that was the problem of it being manifested in the Tanakh. A lot of what we read in the Tanakh was still for people there willing to come to YAHUAH and the Torah to receive rivers of flowing living water. The word is life; however, we read here, and it says, the Spirit has not yet been; so, He is also speaking of a time that has not come. Zechariah states that it has not come; Act 2 did not fulfill all of this; it was part of it, no doubt, but it is not really what it is talking about. It is just scratching the surface; the fullness of it does not come until you read Revelation 21 and 22; that is what we are being hinted at in chapter 7 of Revelation. It matches up with Zechariah during the end times battles; there will be those that are going to find their way to the rivers of living water; this is what this is all about. This is the connection to the Spirit that we are connecting back to in John chapter 6, where He said, "My words are Spirit." We also see a connection that the words in the Torah are also essentially the rivers of living water.

You can drink without paying; it is available to you free; drink as much as you want; I encourage you to drink a lot of it every day. When He says, give us this day; our daily bread; well, He says, I am the bread of life. He gives you all kinds of metaphors in the forms of eating and drinking; it talks about famines of the word and people being hungry. He talks about the problem with thirstiness, and they will not thirst anymore. It is all about Him, the Spirit of truth talked about in John 14; He says, I am the truth and the Spirit of truth I will be with you, stay with you, and be in you. However, that is only going to stay, if you stay in Him; stay in the Torah; the word; the truth. Again, He says, my words are the Spirit of truth. It is what the Spirit is; it is not a person; it is the way that a being, known as; the Son; interacts with us and transfers information to us; feeds us, when we are hungry, we eat of his body. When we are thirsty, He gives us drink; we drink of his blood; and blood symbolizes for us life, as life is in the blood. We read this in the Tanakh; the Old Testament; the life in the blood. This is why we are told not to drink physical blood literally. When He says to drink of my blood; He is saying drink My life or drink My word because out of Me flows rivers of living water. Those who have been studying Torah know it is like a torrent; there are rivers of this that is overflowing; it knocks you down; it can be like drinking out of a firehose.

Hopefully, it will wash out and knock over every paradigm that you have got wrong; every idea, every doctrinal position, understanding, and error that is in your system. It will wash it all out; you know you have to take it in to wash it out; you need to go through a cleansing. That cleansing begins with the scriptures; the book; drink His word; His word is life. There is your connection for understanding the Spirit; one of the aspects of the Spirit is it leads to life; it is going to help you to understand the words of life. It will help you connect, understand, and bring them to your memory. Of course, you have to be submissive to it; it is going to grieve the Ruach if every time the Ruach tries to show you something you ignore it. So, when you say, grieving the Ruach, we are not saying the Spirit itself is grieving; the Ruach is an extension of the Father and the Son. When you grieve the Spirit, you are grieving the one who is trying to talk to you; reach you; to do something with you. We will explore this in the next chapter. Above all, you will now understand this connection; this paradigm shift will make more sense; you cannot point to the verse that says, the Spirit had not come yet; assuming it is talking about Acts 2 and then say that was the fulfillment of this entire thing. Everything that we read about that event has not happened yet. The Prophet says it has not happened yet; Revelation; John; they all say it has not happened yet. It was a piece of it; a drop in the bucket, so to speak. Ultimately what YAHUSHUA is talking about in John is something that is going to be an ongoing thing until Revelation; until new Jerusalem and the new earth.

PRAYER

Father, we come before you, and Father we want to thank you for giving us your Ruach. For pouring forth the understanding that we need of your word through the Spirit; that the Spirit helps to bring to understanding. That is the way that you share information with us; that is the way that you transfer information to us; the way you speak to us; through the Ruach. Father, help us that we might be submissive to your voice through that means. Father, we are so hungry and thirsty to eat of the bread of life and to drink of the rivers of living water. Father, we know the only thing that is stopping us is us. Father, help us to do what we need to do to get out of the way and submit; lay down all that self-sovereignty stuff and all of those filters. Help us to truly understand your word and be able to have a clear conduit between you and us; clear up any static that is preventing our connection. Father, please help us to stop the things that are causing static and distraction; hampering your ability to reach us and talk to us. Help us to listen and find life; we know that it is your desire that we would live and not die. So, Father, we thank you for the insight and the understanding; for your words and for giving it as the written word; so that we could understand what you would have us to understand. Thank you for the Spirit, for helping us to unlock the understanding of those words; to put them into the pieces of the puzzle and to put it together so that we can know what your will is. Allow us to be pleasing in your sight; we thank you; we praise you; we appreciate all the work that you are doing in our lives in submission to the authority of our coming Savior; our coming King; our high priest YAHUSHUA Ha Mashiach; it is in His authority and His name that we come to you in agreement we say; AMEN .

THE SWORD

Let us begin in Ephesians 6:11,17, we are talking about what the Ruach Ha Kodesh was, and what it is. We are told in verse 11, "Put on the whole armor of ELOHIM, that ye may be able to stand against the wiles of the devil." Now, let us read verse 17, it says, "And take the helmet of salvation, and the sword of the Spirit, which is the word of ELOHIM:" Remember, that the Spirit of the Ruach is not a third entity; it is not part of a Trinity. Here is says, that the word of ELOHIM is Spirit; which is consistent with what we have been showing you. Go to verse 18; we are to take the sword of the Spirit, which is the word of ELOHIM, "Praying always with all prayer and supplication in the Spirit, and watching thereunto with all perseverance and supplication for all saints;" Now, the Charismatics will often use verse eighteen without using verse seventeen; when it says, "...praying in the word of ELOHIM..."; the previous verse explains that verse. You cannot just read verse eighteen by itself. It is the word of ELOHIM, he says, the sword of the Spirit which is the word of ELOHIM. We are to pray in the context of the word of ELOHIM; that is an entirely different perspective; however, it is completely consistent with everything we have been showing you from the word in this series. What is the word of ELOHIM? YAHUSHUA is the word of ELOHIM; we know the word put on flesh (John 1:14), we also know that the word is truth; YAHUSHUA is truth; we understand that the word is, and the truth is the Torah. The Torah is the word; the instructions; so, it says here that we are to pray in supplication. Supplicating ourselves to what the truth; the word; the Messiah; the Torah is. It is not some separate thing we cannot grasp on to; it is consistent from the previous verse; all of this is in the context of what putting on the armor is; so that we can stand against the schemes of the devil. Look at verse 12, it reads, "For we wrestle not against flesh and blood, but against principalities, against powers, against the rulers of the darkness of this world, against spiritual wickedness in high places." How do we fight against that? The truth, the Torah; YAHUSHUA. This is all flowing into the ending where He goes through the different pieces of armor, and after he gives the last part; with the helmet of deliverance (Salvation) and the sword of the Spirit; He says, then we can take out most effective weapon, and pray at all times in the context of the word of ELOHIM. By being supplicated to that word; submissive to that word. Now, hopefully, that cleared up some things that maybe you did not always understand the context of verse eighteen. Let us continue, go to Mark 13:9-11, let us look at some of the things that the Ruach does, "But take heed to yourselves: for they shall deliver you up to councils; and in the synagogues ye shall be beaten: and ye shall be brought before rulers and kings for My sake, for a testimony against them." Verse 10, "And the gospel must first be published among all nations." Verse 11, "But when they shall lead you, and deliver you up, take no thought beforehand what ye shall speak, neither do ye premeditate: but whatsoever shall be given you in that hour, that speak ye: for it is not ye that speak, but the set-apart Spirit." It is not like you are going to be possessed; we think of possession as the only thing that happens on the negative side. If you are submissive, get out of the way, and you will be in a place for a direct download, allow inspiration; the stirring to remembrance; the bringing forth of everything that He has already given you.

So, if you try not to have any preconceptions of how this is going to look, get out of the way and allow the Ruach to lead. If you could be submissive and trust the Ruach; the Spirit will give you the words; they will pour forth out of your mouth. The Spirit gives us the words to speak. The Spirit also gives us power and boldness to preach the truth. Go to Acts 4:29-31, it reads, "And now, YAHUAH, behold their threatenings: and grant unto thy servants, that with all boldness they may speak thy word," Verse 30, "By stretching forth thine hand to heal; and that signs and wonders may be done by the name of Thy holy child YAHUSHUA." Verse 31, "And when they had prayed, the place was shaken where they were assembled together; and they were all filled with the set-apart Spirit, and they spake the word of ELOHIM with boldness." Again, this is the most powerful manifestation; being filled with the Ruach is not necessarily the idea of speaking in different tongues. It is speaking the word of ELOHIM with boldness; you see this with Moses and the seventy elders. When the Spirit that was on him was put on them, what did they do? They started speaking the word of ELOHIM with boldness; of course, Joshua got offended and jealous, and said to his mentor Moses, make them stop. Moses said, he wished everybody was doing it; Paul says the same thing; he wished everybody would prophesize. Prophecy is speaking the word of ELOHIM with boldness; it is not speaking the future, necessarily, although it does have that element of it occasionally, that is not the primary purpose of prophecy. A prophet is the one who speaks with authority, the word of ELOHIM, that is the scriptural definition. He is saying here, when they were filled with the Ruach, they spoke the word of ELOHIM with boldness; you want to be able to speak with boldness; they prayed; they believed; they trusted.

When it says they were filled, I am going to say that is not necessarily the conclusion here; they had none of it before; now, we all have a little taste of it; we are talking about being immersed in it. John the Baptist said, I baptize you in water, but the one who is coming will baptize you; immerse you in the Spirit and fire. Immersed means to be filled to overflowing; to be surrounded by the Spirit. We are not going to assume that these people had not, but they were filled with; immersed in the Spirit. He came through their belief, trust, prayer, and commitment. So, with what did they receive as the fruit to speak the word of ELOHIM? Boldness.

Now, turn to 2 Timothy 1:6-7, reads, " Wherefore I put thee in remembrance that thou stir up the gift of ELOHIM, which is in thee by the putting on of my hands." Verse 7, "For ELOHIM hath not given us the spirit of fear; but of power, and of love, and of a sound mind." This is still talking about His Spirit that He gave us, which again, it does not fit in here a third person or an entity. It has to do with the intrinsic nature of ELOHIM. He connects to us and fills us; transfers his nature through this thing called the Ruach of the Spirit. He is saying here; I would want to remind you to stir up this gift of ELOHIM which is in you, through the laying on of hands. Now, the laying on of hands is not this magical thing of putting my hands on you.

The fact that Paul was able to lay his hands; grab ahold of these people and teach them; get them to where they needed to be. It was not a ceremonial laying on of hands; could it be that Paul is saying to Timothy, I want to remind you to stir up the gift that is in you; through the fact that you submitted to me in a discipleship process. You let me lay my hands on you and grab ahold of you; walk you through this process to where you are right now. That is an entirely different way as opposed to a preacher put his hands on you with oil. This is a discipleship process, a person volunteers to allow the mentor to lay hands on him; to grab ahold of him, and set him straight; to teach; instruct him in the way he should go. What 2 Timothy is saying is, for this reason, I remind you to stir up the gift that you have in you through the laying of my hands; I guided you through the process to receive this gift.

ELOHIM has not given us a Spirit of cowardice, but of power, love, and of self-control. Do not be ashamed of using it. Paul says in verse 8 to go forth consistently with what we have already read with boldness to preach the word. Some people have their agenda when it comes to the laying of hands; the only one who wins is the enemy. He gets everybody to think the process is wrong. No, the process is right the people implementing the process were wrong. If you read the scriptures, you see the process; do not throw it out because it was poorly done.

Continuing to Ephesians 2:18, reads, "For through him we both have access by one Spirit unto the Father." We have access to the Father through this thing that I call, "the means by which." One of the aspects of the Spirit is it gives us access to the Father, it is, "the means by which," we communicate with Him; it is how He gets what He gets done. It is not like we have to go through this third entity of the Trinity, and this is how we access the father; that is not what it is saying here. He says because through Him. Who is through Him? YAHUSHUA. Look at verse 19, it says, "Now, therefore, ye are no more strangers and foreigners, but fellow-citizens with the saints, and of the household of ELOHIM;" We all have the same Spirit that makes us no longer strangers to the covenant we had broken before as Israelites. Again, remember, this is all about one bloodline so, if the people in that bloodline all have the potential to have the same Spirit; that is what makes us no longer strangers. How do we have the same Spirit through Him; Through YAHUSHUA the Messiah of Israel. We have the same Spirit. Go to verses 20-22, it reads, "And are built upon the foundation of the apostles and prophets, YAHUSHUA Messiah himself being the chief cornerstone;" Verse 21, "In whom all the building fitly framed together groweth unto an holy temple in ELOHIM:" Verse 22, "In whom ye also are builded together for an habitation of ELOHIM through the Spirit." That is what makes us family; citizens together of New Jerusalem to come. What is the Spirit?

The word of ELOHIM; you are saying it is "the means by which," He brings us all together; it is His intrinsic nature; ELOHIM is Spirit; He is trying to give us His full embodiment of who and what He is; He is trying to transfer that to you; in changing your character, heart, and mind to be like him. To turn His people into the embodiment of Himself as his wife in the Kingdom. Continuing on, go to Romans 5:1-2, it reads, "Therefore being justified by faith, we have peace with ELOHIM through our Master YAHUSHUA Ha Mashiach:" Verse 2, "By whom also we have access by faith into this grace wherein we stand, and rejoice in hope of the glory of ELOHIM." He says we have "access"; when we see the word "access", what should we be thinking about? The Ruach. The Ruach is what gives us access, but what gives us the ability to use the Ruach? Our belief. He says, by our belief, we have this process, so, we believe then we are filled with the Ruach, and we have access. Read verses 3-5, it says, "And not only so, but we glory in tribulations also: knowing that tribulation worketh patience;" Verse 4, "And patience, experience; and experience, hope:" Verse 5, "And hope maketh not ashamed; because the love of ELOHIM is shed abroad in our hearts by the set-apart Spirit which is given unto us."

Now we see that the Ruach has brought us into this in verse 5; it is in the context of the entire script; he says we go for this process, but then as we are going through it; we end up under pressure, which then goes into the parable of the sower of the seed. You are going to have things try to choke out and mess with you depending on how good your ground is; here it is saying we must exalt YAHUAH in these pressures; this is the baptism of fire. The fire tests and purifies you; it puts you through that kind of heat that is going to see what is there; see what you are made of; He says as you go through that process, His expectation does not disappoint. That expectation is not going to disappoint if you endure through the pressures; it says, and it does not disappoint because the love of ELOHIM has been poured out in our hearts. How? By the Ruach Ha Kodesh, which was given to us. It again, is that access that keeps communicating to you; that still small voice, saying hang in there, do not give up, do not quit, endure until the end. It says - he who overcomes till the end, will receive all the blessings. Everything in your scriptures leads eventually to the revelation that says, and unto he who overcomes till the end will receive all this; that is the bottom line. So, through the Spirit, the love of ELOHIM is poured out into our hearts; ELOHIM is love, but the Torah teaches us how to love Him and how to love our neighbor. After all, what are the two great commands? How to love Him and how to love each other; how do we do that? His other instructions tell us how to do that. Go to Ephesians 3:14-16, "For this cause I bow my knees unto the Father of our master YAHUSHUA Messiah," Verse 15, "Of whom the whole family in heaven and earth is named," Verse 16, "That He would grant you, according to the riches of His glory, to be strengthened with might by His Spirit in the inner man;" So, the Ruach is supposed to strengthen your inner man. The Spirit is the word of the ELOHIM; the word is supposed to strengthen your inner man. It is not going to do any of that if you do not spend any time reading, studying, and embracing it. Making it a part of you; it is going to strengthen the inner man. Moving on, go to verse 17, it reads, "That Messiah may dwell in your hearts by faith; that ye, being rooted and grounded in love," He is connecting here what we already read in John 14. He is linking this Spirit in verse 16 to the Messiah himself; He says to be strengthened in the inner man through His Spirit, that the Messiah might dwell in your hearts through belief. If you do not believe, it is not going to happen; how do I know? Again, John 14; it says, if you love me, keep my commands; then I will send you the Spirit. So, belief is linked to this entire thing; having then been rooted and grounded in love. You can take that word love, and change it to Torah; YAHUSHUA; all of that is what love is; in order that you; verses 18-19, "May be able to comprehend with all saints what is the breadth, and length, and depth, and height;" Verse 19, "And to know the love of Messiah, which passeth knowledge, that ye might be filled with all the fulness of ELOHIM."

In other words, that you might become entirely like Him, but it is going to take all of the steps we have shown you up to this point in the previous three series. It is going to take you to the point of belief and trust where you submit to the instructions through the Ruach; the Spirit. Look at verse 20-21, "Now unto him, that is able to do exceeding abundantly above all that we ask or think, according to the power that worketh in us," Verse 21, "Unto him be glory in the church by Messiah YAHUSHUA throughout all ages, world without end. Amen." Hopefully, you have a good grasp on what the Ruach is; but what is it we need to do? After all, that is the most important thing to us; all this information is good, but what is expected from us; what is it that we are supposed to do; how does this whole thing play out in terms of us, so, that we could be pleasing in His sight. Let us go back now to the beginning; go to Genesis 6:3, it reads, "And the YAHUAH said, My spirit shall not always strive with man, for that he also is flesh: yet his days shall be an hundred and twenty years." So, for everybody that wants to hear the teachings that are out there saying that nobody in the Old Testament had the Spirit; verse 3 disagrees with you, (along with another 500 verses disagree with you as well), but it is undoubtedly right here in Genesis it says my Spirit shall not strive with man forever. He said, my Spirit is striving with him right now; it is not going to be like that forever. Again, what is His Spirit? The word of ELOHIM; so, the man was striving against what YAHUAH said, to do and not do. See, we have the Bible start defining itself; we know that the word of ELOHIM is what the Spirit is; a Spirit as the word of ELOHIM. He says my word, my teachings; my instructions shall not strive with man forever. My intrinsic nature is not going to strive with effort; I am going to get 120 years; I am not going to give him forever if he wants not to listen, and strive against me; he has 120 years. Now, turn to Matthew 5:3, let us build on the same thing, this is part of the Beatitudes, as they call him; the blessed czar, it reads, "Blessed are the poor in spirit: for theirs is the kingdom of heaven." The word, "poor," in the Greek, again we are hampered against truly understanding scripture because the translations are so awful. So, the word, "poor," does not give us the right understanding, unless you are going to think of the poor as a picture of a poor person begging. This is talking about blessed are those who are begging for the Ruach. It also could be turned on a second understanding; remember Hebraically things are not either/or, but both; blessed are those who are poor in their own Spirit and then they are going to seek out and beg for His Spirit. Realize that the Greek word in this verse is better said, they are trying to picture the idea of one who is begging. So, what is the Spirit of the word of ELOHIM? Those who are hungry and thirsty for the word; so, it is consistent. Praise ABBA that His word is consistent if we read it for what it says; it is man that makes it confusing.

Now, let us take that same understanding and read Psalm 51:15-17, " O YAHUAH, open thou my lips; and my mouth shall shew forth thy praise." Verse 16, "For thou desirest not sacrifice; else would I give it: thou delightest not in burnt offering." Verse 17, "The sacrifices of ELOHIM are a broken spirit: a broken and a contrite heart, O YAHUAH, thou wilt not despise." That is the "Blessed are," in verse 3 of Matthew that YAHUSHUA was talking about; blessed are those that are in Psalm 51:17. What does broken Spirit mean? It means the Spirit in man has been broken; so that now the Spirit of ELOHIM can go in; think of it like a wild stallion; a horse. What do they have to do with those mustangs; they have to break them before they can be of any use. Some of you may say, my life is fine; well, maybe He is still trying to break you, and you are not letting Him. Let Him break you so that He can build you back up; stop holding on with that strong tenacity that you will not let go of. Quickly go to James 4:8-10, "Draw nigh to ELOHIM, and he will draw nigh to you. Cleanse your hands, ye sinners; and purify your hearts, ye double minded." Verse 9, "Be afflicted, and mourn, and weep: let your laughter be turned to mourning and your joy to heaviness." Verse 10, "Humble yourselves in the sight of the master, and he shall lift you up." So, what is he talking about? He is saying, get over it; do what you have to do; yell, kick, scream about the stuff that you have to give up, and humble yourselves; He can lift you up. It is the same as Psalm 51 and Matthew 5; they are saying the same thing; you have to allow Him to break you and get it done, so, you can be free and lifted up. Let Him mold you as the master potter, into the image He wants to mold.

Moving on, go to 1 Peter 1:1, "Peter, an apostle of YAHSHUA Messiah , to the strangers scattered throughout Pontus, Galatia, Cappadocia, Asia, and Bithynia," He is writing to those who were scattered; the lost Israelites; the 10 tribes; he is saying to those people; the chosen who are strangers of the dispersion. Verse 2, "Elect according to the foreknowledge of ELOHIM the Father, through sanctification of the Spirit, unto obedience and sprinkling of the blood of YAHUSHUA Messiah: Grace unto you, and peace, be multiplied." Those in the dispersion that is set-apart for obedience; why? Because this is the simplicity of the Covenant at Exodus 19; you agree to obey, and I will agree to take you as my people. The Covenant is not a complicated document. The details are many, but the details are very simply based on, you already said you would obey; now He is going to tell you what you need to obey. You need to obey these things, and then I will take you as my people; here are those who are prophesied to be scattered and to be regathered and he said, look you were warned; there was foreknowledge of ELOHIM; the Father knew that you would be out there. Remember, one part of the good news is that the regathering has begun; it is not just the good news the YAHUSHUA died, was buried, and was resurrected for the salvation of His people the Israelites; that is really good news, but the good news that everybody talks about is what they have been waiting for; the prophesied redemption and return at a dispersion. So, again in verse 2, he is saying, "Elect according to the foreknowledge of ELOHIM the Father, through sanctification of the Spirit, unto obedience and sprinkling of the blood of YAHUSHUA Messiah: Grace unto you, and peace be multiplied." That only works if you are set-apart to obedience.

It is the Spirit that gives you the strength and the boldness, and the encouragement to be obedient; that is one of the other elements of what the Ruach does for us. Let us continue, go to 1 Corinthians 2:1, we need to have some context; this is why we are starting in verse 1, we are going to read the entire chapter. Verse 1," And I, brethren, when I came to you, came not with excellency of speech or of wisdom, declaring unto you the testimony of ELOHIM." Verse 2, "For I determined not to know anything among you, save YAHUSHUA Messiah, and him crucified." Verse 3, "And I was with you in weakness, and in fear, and in much trembling." Verse 4, "And my speech and my preaching was not with enticing words of man's wisdom, but in demonstration of the Spirit and of power:" Verse 5, "That your faith should not stand in the wisdom of men, but in the power of ELOHIM." Is this not consistent with everything that we have already discussed? Do not worry about what you are going to say and get your agenda out of the way; do not try to be skilled and talented or work it all out in advance; He says I came to you, and I let the Ruach speak through Me to you; by me being weak and getting out of the way; not being strong and dominate trying to show everybody how smart I am.

Moving to verse 6-10, reads, "Howbeit we speak wisdom among them that are perfect: yet not the wisdom of this world, nor of the princes of this world, that come to nought:" Verse 7, "But we speak the wisdom of ELOHIM in a mystery, even the hidden wisdom, which ELOHIM ordained before the world unto our glory:" Verse 8, "Which none of the princes of this world knew: for had they known it, they would not have crucified the master of glory." Verse 9, "But as it is written, Eye hath not seen, nor ear heard, neither have entered into the heart of man, the things which ELOHIM hath prepared for them that love him." Verse 10, "But ELOHIM hath revealed them unto us by his Spirit: for the Spirit searcheth all things, yea, the deep things of ELOHIM. Remember, one of the things the Ruach does is goes and takes all the pieces of the puzzle that you have put in your head by reading and studying the word, and connects the dots. Not only connects them together, but connects them as needed, in other words, when you need something those will be the particular dots that get put together; as you have need if you submit to Him and study the word; allow Him; He will bring the verses together that you needed to understand in order to move forward. Verse 11, reads, "For what man knoweth the things of a man, save the spirit of man which is in him? Even so, the things of ELOHIM knoweth no man, but the Spirit of ELOHIM. He communicates with us by downloading to us; transfers information to us. Verse 12, "Now we have received, not the spirit of the world, but the spirit which is of ELOHIM; that we might know the things that are freely given to us of ELOHIM. Where does this third entity of the Trinity fit into that verse?

"...but the spirit which is of ELOHIM; that we might know the things that are freely given to us of ELOHIM." It does not make sense that it is a being; it is a transfer from Him to you through this, "means by which," Verses 13-14, "Which things also we speak, not in the words which man's wisdom teacheth, but which the set-apart Spirit teacheth; comparing spiritual things with spiritual." Verse 14, "But the natural man receiveth, not the things of the Spirit of ELOHIM: for they are foolishness unto him: neither can he know them because they are spiritually discerned." Like when your family members laugh at you when you want to keep Shabbat; stop eating pork, and not do Christmas or Easter.

All those things they cannot discern, but if the Ruach were working there, it would all be clear; like it became clear to you when He first grabbed ahold of you. Remember, He said none comes lest the Father draws; He also said, none can know the Father unless I reveal Him; so, it has got to go both ways. The Father must reveal the Son, and the Son must reveal the Father; that is how the process works. We do not have the ability to figure this out by our self; we can read the words, but we will not understand because it still will be foolishness without them doing the eye-opening, ear-opening, and heart-opening.

Which is why we have a lot of friends and family that are Israelite by blood, that are very well-read, very well-informed, and still cannot see anything because the Most High has not drawn them to him. It is not their fault; so, no, we do not want to mock or laugh at them. You were them not too long ago; be careful about laughing. Moving on, verses, 15-16, reads, "But he that is spiritual judgeth all things, yet he himself is judged of no man." Verse 16, "For who hath known the mind of the YAHUAH, that he may instruct him? but we have the mind of Messiah." Remember, in Philippians 2:5; it says, "...let this mind be in you, that was in Messiah..." What was this mind? He said, everything the Father says, I do. That's His mind; there is nothing I do that the Father did not tell me to do; I only do what is pleasing in His mind. We are supposed to have that mind.

Go to Galatians 6:8, it reads, "For he that soweth to his flesh shall of the flesh reap corruption; but he that soweth to the Spirit shall of the Spirit reap life everlasting." So, he who sew to the word of ELOHIM shall reap everlasting life from the word of ELOHIM. What is the word of ELOHIM? The truth; the Torah; the life; YAHUSHUA; the Messiah, you see, plug it all in. Does it not get simpler when you know how to do that? All those words are

interchangeable, and not just interchangeable, but they encompass all of those things at the same time. In other words, the word means all of those things; when you see any one of those words in the scriptures, it means all of them. It is all the same; it is all together; how can I say all those words are together because I can show you all the verses that link them together. For instance: John 14, I am the truth; Psalm 119 says, the Torah is the truth; John 1 says, that the word of the Torah put on flesh. Let us continue, go to John 14:15-16, we have read this before, but I want to make sure we understand this. It reads, " If ye love me, keep my commandments." Now, verse 16 flows from verse 15; there is no time-lapse; it does not take place three days later or in a different month. Verse 16, "And I will pray the Father, and he shall give you another Comforter, that he may abide with you forever;" So, does that mean that everybody out there that claims belief in Him gets filled with the Comforter? He says, no. If you love me and keep my commandments; I am going to ask the Father to send you the Comforter; to stay with you forever. What is this Comforter? We addressed this before earlier in the series. It says in verse 17, "Even the Spirit of truth; whom the world cannot receive, because it seeth him not, neither knoweth him: but ye know him; for he dwelleth with you, and shall be in you." The Comforter is the Spirit of truth. Jump back to verse 6, He says, I am the truth; so, it is the Spirit of YAHUSHUA, the Spirit of the truth whom the world is unable to receive because it does not see Him or know Him. However, you already know Him because he stays with you and be in you in the future. Who is He talking about? Himself. In case you are not clear; let us read verse 18, "I will not leave you comfortless: I will come to you."
This is not a third entity; He is talking about a way for Himself to be with you; a way for Himself to fill you; a way for Himself to be inside you. He says I am not going to leave you comfortless; remember, He is saying this to a bunch of Hebrew Israelites that still had not embraced the fact that He was going to die. They still could not receive that; He tried. So, now He was trying to say in verse 19, "Yet a little while, and the world seeth me no more; but ye see me: because I live, ye shall live also." He is trying to explain something they would not grab, but He knew when it happened, they would finally get it. He is trying to say look I have to go away, and they are saying, where are you going, we will come with you. He is saying, no, you do not get it; I have told you over and over, they are going to arrest me, they are going to scourge me, they are going to kill me. They are saying, oh no, be kind to

yourself master; do not say those things; you are not going to die. So, this is information that he has got to get to them; He is saying, do not worry when you see me; I am still going to come to you; I am going to ask the Father to send you the Comforter. The process here for us is to keep His Commandments. All of the is predicated on, "if you love me..." we say we love Him, well then keep His Commandments. Let us keep moving, go to Acts 5:32, it reads, "And we are his witnesses of these things; and so is also the set-apart Ruach, whom ELOHIM hath given to them that obey Him." No verse says if you are not obeying Him; He fills you with a Spirit. That does not mean you have none; everybody has an earnest, but you are not being filled when you are sitting in Sunday Church; doing Christmas and Easter, eating pork. Here it is, this is Peter, "And we are his witnesses of these things; and so is also the Holy Ghost, whom YAHUAH hath given to them that obey Him." Is this not consistent with John 14? Same words, if you love; you keep My Commandments, and then I will send the Spirit. This is what the scriptures say; it is not my fault that you have been lied to. Get mad at the system that has lied to all of us. Telling us were in the truth, and we are not; some of what they teach is the truth, but this is the book talking; let us listen to what Peter says and do not worry so much about what you think.

Let us move on to Luke 11:9; remember we are talking about our process in this; obedience is a big part of it. It reads, "And I say unto you, Ask, and it shall be given you; seek, and ye shall find; knock, and it shall be opened unto you." Verse 10, "For every one that asketh receiveth; and he that seeketh findeth; and to him that knocketh it shall be opened." Verse 11, "If a son shall ask bread of any of you that is a father, will he give him a stone? or if he ask a fish, will he for a fish give him a serpent? "Verse 12, "Or if he shall ask an egg, will he offer him a scorpion?" Verse 13, "If ye then, being evil, know how to give good gifts unto your children: how much more shall your heavenly Father give the set-apart Spirit to them that ask him?"

What is our role? To ask, seek, and knock; that is not sitting there saying, give me more of your Spirit; give me more experience. It is willing to say, how do I do it? What do you expect for me to get more of your Spirit? What is it you require? Not setting there saying, give me. How about saying, I need this; I know I need this; I am asking, seeking, and knocking. I need to understand what is it that is required of me to get my birth right. How about obedience. Obedience is required. So, we have to ask, seek, and knock; but we are also asking for the path; the process; what is the path to this? Let us move on to John 4:23-24, "But the hour cometh, and now is when the true worshippers shall worship the Father in spirit and in truth: for the Father seeketh such to worship him." Verse 24, "ELOHIM is a Spirit: and they that worship him must worship him in spirit and in truth." He is seeking those who will worship Him in Spirit; What is Spirit? The word of ELOHIM; truth; What is truth? YAHUSHUA's the truth. So, it has got to be both; together. Remember, truth is the mechanics of it and the Spirit is the fullness of the intent. For example: In Matthew, it says do not commit adultery, but is say do not even lust in your heart to do it; that is Spirit and truth. The Spirit of it; the intent of it; the fullness of how it was intended. See, ELOHIM is the goal of the entire thing; to be like ELOHIM; to be like YAHUSHUA; if you do these things you become more and more like them, so, He is seeking those that will worship in Spirit and truth. It does not mean in a babbling language or an ethereal mantra; it means to do it in the word of ELOHIM, in the way He intended it to be done; in the mechanics of it; that is the Spirit. Many people are looking for emotional stuff; it has nothing to do with what He is talking about here; He is not saying you need to worship Him, emotionalism, and truth. He is saying; you need to do this with all the mechanics in place; how it was intended.

Doing the mechanical part and not having your heart behind it will result in you getting laid low in the desert, so to speak. Doing it with all the right intent is essential; not begrudgingly, whining, and complaining about it. We have to be careful of the definition of the Spirit. He says the word of ELOHIM is Spirit. Moving on, go to Matthew 12:24-31, let us find out about this idea of blaspheming against the Spirit; grieving the Spirit, and that kind to thing. Verse 24, "But when the Pharisees heard it, they said, This fellow doth not cast out devils, but by Beelzebub the prince of the devils." Verse 25, "And YAHUSHUA knew their thoughts, and said unto them, Every kingdom divided against itself is brought to desolation; and every city or house divided against itself shall not stand:" Verse 26, "And if Satan cast out Satan, he is divided against himself; how shall then his kingdom stand?" Verse 27, "And if I by Beelzebub cast out devils, by whom do your children cast them out? therefore they shall be your judges." Verse 28, "But if I cast out devils by the Spirit of ELOHIM, then the kingdom of ELOHIM is come unto you." Verse 29, "Or else how can one enter into a strong man's house, and spoil his goods, except he first bind the strong man? and then he will spoil his house." Continuing, Verse 30, "He that is not with Me is against Me; and he that gathereth not with Me scattereth abroad." Now, before we read the rest of the verse, because of everything He said about a house divided; let us keep the context in mind. Verse 31, "Wherefore I say unto you, All manner of sin and blasphemy shall be forgiven unto men: but the blasphemy against the set-apart Spirit shall not be forgiven unto men." Verse 32, "And whosoever speaketh a word against the Son of man, it shall be forgiven him: but whosoever speaketh against the Ruach Ha Kodesh, it shall not be forgiven him, neither in this world, neither in the world to come." So, speaking against the Spirit; what is speaking against the Spirit? What did we say was the word of ELOHIM? How about telling everybody that the word was done away with; that the word was nailed to the cross; that the word does not apply. Also, blaspheme; saying things like; by the power of the Ruach and being in complete consistency with His Father is casting out demons, and giving credit to a being, Beelzebub. Look at the context leading into this; how do you blaspheme; you give credit to the enemy for that which is of the Father. You cannot see it as of the Father; some people will tell you; you are mocking YAHUSHUA by keeping the Commandments; because you are trying to keep the Torah. What saves them is that they are doing it, not knowing what they are doing; that is the only thing that gives them an opportunity. They are doing what they were taught to do. Remembering who He is speaking to here; the Pharisees, who should have known better. The context here is vital; who is talking to? The Pharisees; that is His audience. He is telling them this will not be forgiven because you should know better; you are blaspheming against the Ruach. When He talks about this blasphemy against the Spirit, it is all in the context of what happened before. They were giving Beelzebub credit for something that the Father was doing through YAHUSHUA. That is the context; He says in verse 31, because of this; what is this? The house divided against itself. What is the house divided against itself stuff? All the Commandments are nailed to the cross; the Israelites blew it, and now it is everyone who believes in YASUSHUA's turn; all this replacement theology stuff, People saying they they are the 2nd coming of YAHUSHUA, people saying that the spirit told them that next week the world is going to end; that is what he is saying is blaspheming against the Ruach. Anything that does not line up with scriptures, that the person or organization knows is a lie or has been told the truth and continues to push that lie is blaspheming of the Ruach.

All of the people out there trying to tell you; you do not have to keep everything; they ought to be scared of what is going on in this verse. They are not because they have bent and twisted a bunch of verses out of the book of Hebrews and Galatians to give excused to say that the Torah was done away with. Now, they are not quite where mainstream Christianity is saying all of it was done away with; which by the way, they do not believe it either; because I have spoken to a mainstream Christian; so, the commandments are done away with? Yes, they are. I said, fine, so, if your wife gets raped, killed, and all your stuff is stolen; is that okay? No. Well, you said the law was done away with; the Torah is done away with; so, why would you have a problem with that; there is no law against it; you told me you do not believe in the Commandments. Why would you have a problem with that? Well, no those are laws.

On the same list of laws is keeping the Sabbath; in fact, it sits in the top four which if you notice are how we are supposed to love the Father. The last 6 of murder, adultery; that are lower down are how we are to love our fellow Israelites; Do you understand? The 2 commandments that YAHUSHUA spoke about break down the 10 commandments that then break down the 613 commandments. So, blasphemy of the Spirit has a lot to do with it; if not all. The idea here, at least in Matthew when YAHUSHUA was talking about a house divided against itself and giving credit to the enemy for that which is of the Father. Again, it was being spoken to those who should have known better. If you are in a place where you should know better; you should be terrified. This is why being a teacher of the word has so much responsibility but remember, to whom much is given, much is expected.

Let us go now to Ephesians 4:17-27, "This I say therefore, and testify in YAHUAH, that ye henceforth walk not as other Gentiles walk, in the vanity of their mind," Verse 18, "Having the understanding darkened, being alienated from the life of ELOHIM through the ignorance that is in them, because of the blindness of their heart:" Verse 19, "Who being past feeling have given themselves over unto lasciviousness, to work all uncleanness with greediness." Verse 20, "But ye have not so learned Messiah;" Verse 21, "If so be that ye have heard him, and have been taught by him, as the truth is in YAHUSHUA:" Verse 22, "That ye put off concerning the former conversation the old man, which is corrupt according to the deceitful lusts;" Continuing, verse 23, "And be renewed in the spirit of your mind;" Verse 24, "And that ye put on the new man, which after ELOHIM is created in righteousness and true holiness." Verse 25, "Wherefore putting away lying, speak every man truth with his neighbour: for we are members one of another." Verse 26, "Be ye angry, and sin not: let not the sun go down upon your wrath:" Verse 27, "Neither give place to the devil." As we are going through all of this; we are setting the context to the verse I want to get to about grieving the Spirit. We have to know all this context before we get there. He said, nor give place to the devil. Verses 28-30, "Let him that stole steal no more: but rather let him labour, working with his hands the thing which is good, that he may have to give to him that needeth." Verse 29, "Let no corrupt communication proceed out of your mouth, but that which is good to the use of edifying, that it may minister grace unto the hearers." Verse 30, "And grieve not the holy Spirit of ELOHIM, whereby ye are sealed unto the day of redemption." So, how do we grieve it? By doing all this stuff; what stuff? Walking the futility of your mind; darkening your understanding; hardening your heart; read the previous verses.

If you do all of that; you are going to grieve the Ruach of ELOHIM, by whom you were sealed for the day of redemption, and the reason you grieve the Ruach is that the Ruach wants you to walk in His truth. If the Ruach is now grieved then that makes clear you will not be obtaining the promises and living in New Jerusalem. You are going to choose to go the other way because you have freedom of choice; this laments the Ruach, the Father, and His Spirit. Why would you choose to walk in futility and do all these horrible, corrupt, unclean things? That is how you grieve the Spirits; not real complicated; go back to chapter 4:1 and understand what He is talking about. He says, I ask you, and I call upon you to walk worthily of the calling which you are called. In 1 Thessalonians 5:19, it says, "Quench not the Spirit." Doing all this stuff; you do just that; harden your heart, being callous, walking in your ignorance; your futility of your mind. What is the futility of your mind? Thinking you know better; doing something because you believe He is going to be ok with it; you better be right. Saying things like, He knows my heart; yes, He does, but you do not seem to realize that; so, you are trying to spin it so you can walk in the emptiness of your mind. You are going to do it, again and again, and it is never going to get you what you hoped for; wanting to do things your way and thinking He will be ok with it. It does not work that way. Go to 2 Corinthians 5:5, "Now he that hath wrought us for the selfsame thing is ELOHIM, who also hath given unto us the earnest of the Spirit." Now, go to 1 Corinthians 6:20, it reads, "For ye are bought with a price: therefore glorify YAHUAH in your body, and in your spirit, which are

ELOHIM's."

See, so all of us have a piece of the Ruach; of the Spirit; it is an earnest of the payment in full that is to come for Hebrew Israelites; "If", that is the big word; If, you do your part. Here we are talking about this earnest; He says, who has sealed us and gave us Spirit in our hearts as an earnest. Go to 2 Corinthians 1:21-22, " Now he which establisheth us with you in Messiah, and hath anointed us, is ELOHIM;" Verse 22, "Who hath also sealed us, and given the earnest of the Spirit in our hearts." As an earnest. Understand all of us Israelites have the Spirit; every one of us; we are all born with a piece of the Spirit; it is an earnest; it is the connectivity by which He can give you more. To fill you more with the Ruach, which is the whole reason for this series. The idea that John said, the one who is coming is going to immerse you in the Ruach Ha Kodesh; in the Holy Spirit, but you have to participate in that; He is not going to walk over to you and drop it on your head. We have to submit; we have to ask, seek, and knock; we have to do all these things. And then we become a Hebrew which means "one that has crossed over" Israelite which means "Prince of the Power". We become what the Father created us to be as the original creation before the sin of the first Adam.

PRAYER

Father, we come before you, and we so desire to truly understand what you want us to understand about your walk; about your Spirit. Father, help us not just to continue to walk in the futility of our minds; walking in the ignorance and the delusions, and lies that have been given to us about your rule. Help us, Father, to understand that it is your way of interacting with us; it is the means that you use to interact with us; to call us; to talk to us; to draw us; to give us strength and encouragement to whatever it is. That is your way you communicate with us; it is the way you interact with us, and so Father, help us to embrace that and not to take that lightly; we know it is a huge thing. Let us take full advantage of that relational thing that means that you gave us to communicate with you. Also, help us to embrace the requirements that you have given us to say that if we do this, then you will fill us more with your rule; then you will interact with us more give us more understanding; intervene for us; more healing. We understand Father; it is so hard because the Spirit and man struggle and strives as we read earlier; we know you do not want to strive with us; you want us to submit to you. But, Father our Spirits drives; help us to have the courage to put that Spirit down; to break that Spirit; to allow that Spirit to be broken; so, that we will no longer strive against you; but will fully submit to you. So, Father, to do that we ask that you would fill us with your Spirit to strengthen us in obedience; to strengthen us in submission; to strengthen us in doing what pleases you. We that you for your Spirit; we thank you for your wisdom and understanding; we thank you for your Son, YAHUSHUA; we thank you for calling us at this time, and we want to give you glory, and honor for all these things. In the name, and authority of YAHUSHUA, our Messiah. AMEN.